AT THE PRECIPICE OF TIME: THE SEVEN FEASTS

BOOK 1

At the Precipice of Time: The Seven Feasts

© 2021 Gloire Emmanuel Ndongala

Authors contact details:
Email: gloire@gloirendongala.com
Instagram: Gloire777
Website: Gloirendongala.com

ISBN: 978-1-7373259-0-1

Published by
Gloire Emmanuel Ndongala

Table of Contents

To my wife

We're a few years in towards forever, we shifting gears
now together,

Storms we weathered, weather or not, we tied the knot,
and we ain't about to stop.

The top, we're gonna reach the top if we're standing on
the Rock,

Unashamed of His Name, He's got us on lock.

But He's the key and through Him we see, that meant
to be is you and me.

In Him we move and have our being, you're a part of
me like remembering.

In my mind, like life and time, I've memorized your eyes
and found out the greatest prize is you by my side.

You my ride or die; it hasn't all been wonder, but what
God put together let no man put asunder.

Truth is, when God speaks some hear angels,

Others will hear thunder, yet we choose to sit under,

And truly stand; "understand." No longer will we fear man, especially when ignorance is on demand.

Nobody wants instruction; broad is the path to destruction, not saying we're perfect, Lord knows we still under construction.

Roads still being paved, by grace through faith we've been saved,

Amid the world's travesties, what legacy is our love meant leave,

Unity despite scrutiny proves to the world Gods in you and me,

God says He desires it so our children can turn out godly,

Our love though is like when one sows deep below, death occurs and then it grows.

This is what happens when we grab our Bible and live like it's more than a recital.

The flesh may die, but our love will never be idle.

AT THE PRECIPICE OF TIME: THE SEVEN FEASTS

BOOK 1

The Precipice of Time

This then, is where we are, standing on the precipice of time, staring at the stars.

How will things unfold? He's not coming, we're told. Will we all be left in the dark, or will some see what's ahead?

Will you take the mark, or choose Jesus instead?

The time, like the sunlight, will one day fade away; like when we sleep, and eventually must wake.

Tick-Tock goes the clock, one day heavens gates will lock, tell! Tell!

Humanity fell deeper than where lava dwells!

They found themselves headed to hell, Jesus who's the source of eternities well, in love with us He fell and freed humanity from deaths cell,

Now to escape the fiery lake, being known by Jesus is all it takes, do it before time breaks, the earthquakes, and the dead wakes,

Before the mountains shatter, we see Jacob's ladder, and meet the creator of matter,

Before the unknown becomes known and many reap

what they have sown,

Before!

Before there's more and we return to the light we once

wore,

Heaven has only one way in, one must choose Him and

reject sin,

Look at the signs, can't you see all was made by One

who designs, the universe aligns, from planets that

rotate to stars that shine, the precision points to the

One Divine,

Are you part of his Vine? Will He one day tell you, "You

are mine?" We're at the edge of time, some will fall

others will climb,

This is the precipice, either eternal pain, agony, and

restlessness, or love, gain, and fulfillment in God's

premises.

Chapter 1

Signs and Seasons

It has been believed by some scholars and Jewish sages that the book of Genesis holds the key to many of the mysteries of God. To this day, some still believe that the first chapter of Genesis is the bedrock of all of Scripture. It is fitting, therefore, that the word *genesis* begins with *gene*, because in our genes we find our DNA, which hold all the mysteries of who we are and will be.

Just as DNA decoding shows us what an individual can expect in their lifetime, decoding the book of Genesis reveals to us what's to come. When God established the earth, He already knew the future and what would transpire. In Genesis 1:14 we read, "And God said, "Let there be lights in the expanse of the heavens to separate the day from the night. And let them be for signs and for seasons, and for days and years" (ESV).

Why signs? What does this word truly mean? Is there more to the word *seasons* as well? Let us look deeper into the meaning of these words in Hebrew, their original language.

In Hebrew, the word sign is אוֹת Oth, and according to the Brown-Driver-Briggs Lexicon, it means, a signal, evidence, or a mark.[1] Now *seasons*, when plural, is the word מוֹעֲדִים moedim. In its singular form, it would be מוֹעֵד moed, which means a fixed time, season, a signal, an appointed time or feast.

When we put these words together, we can see that God created the stars and planets in the heavens to be a clock. They should be a sign, a warning, a beacon signifying that we are drawing closer to the end. The question is, have we been paying attention to them?

The word *seasons* does not simply imply a time when the weather changes. It is also connected to appointed feasts that God had established. These festivals are distinct in that they are holy convocations (gatherings).

These convocations however were symbolic, as they were preparations for what was to come. They function as dress rehearsals before a wedding ceremony. In other words, every time these feasts occurred, they were supposed to be a signal, a reminder, a sign to us that one day God Himself would assemble with us.

Chapter 2

Leviticus 23: The Rehearsal

There are many different people in the Old Testament whose lives foreshadow Christ. However, there are few who foreshadowed Him greater than Moses. In his final set of instructions to the Israelites, Moses declared,

> "The Lord your God will raise up for you a prophet like me from among you, from your brothers—it is to him you shall listen— just as you desired of the Lord your God at Horeb on the day of the assembly, when you said, 'Let me not hear again the voice of the Lord my God or see this great fire any more, lest I die.' And the Lord said to me, 'They are right in what they have spoken. I will raise up for them a prophet like you from among their brothers. And I will put my words in his mouth, and he shall speak to them all that I command him. And whoever will not listen to my words that he shall speak in my name, I myself will require it of him" (Deuteronomy 18:15-19).

God, through Moses, spoke in this passage of a specific person who would be raised from among the people. This person would be like Moses, a mediator, and a mouthpiece of God.

Jesus is the fulfillment of this prophecy. He was raised up from among the children of Israel and was the Word of God manifested (John 1:1; Hebrews 2:14). Even the Hebrew writer throughout the book of Hebrews compared Jesus' ministry to that of Moses' (Hebrew 3:1-6; Hebrew 7). John also compared Moses to Jesus when he stated,

> *"For the law was given through Moses; grace and truth came through Jesus Christ. No one has ever seen God; the only God, who is at the Father's side, has made him known" (John 1:17-18 ESV).*

Moses in the Old Testament represents a type of Christ. He is someone who foreshadows Him but is not Him. Many of Moses' writings pertained to Christ's ministry, and especially what he wrote in the book of Leviticus.

Therefore, the book of Leviticus is essential if one is to know who Christ is and what He came to do. The ceremonies, the laws, the sacrifices, the garments, the priesthood-almost every single chapter in the book of Leviticus points to Christ (for more insight on this, read the book of Hebrews). It is in Leviticus that we find the seven feasts that God established.

In Leviticus chapter 23, God through Moses spoke about the seven feasts that would be established as a sign forever. In verse two, he said, "Speak to the people of Israel and say to them, 'These are the appointed feasts of the Lord that you shall proclaim as holy convocations; they are my appointed feasts'" (Leviticus 23:1 ESV). Here, we again find the word moedim מוֹעֲדֵי (feasts), which we saw that in Genesis 1:14 was also translated as *seasons*.

These feasts marked the beginning and end of something, just like seasons do. As seasons are fixed and unchanging, so were these feasts. As we prepare for each season differently, God's people, too, were ordered to prepare for each feast accordingly.

What were they preparing for? *To one day meet and be with God.* These feasts all pointed to Jesus Christ's coming, resurrection, and return.

These feasts were broken up into two categories. There are the spring feasts, which consist of The Feast of Passover, The Feast of Unleavened

Bread, The Feast of Firstfruits, and The Feast of Pentecost. This is followed by a three-month gap, summer, when the fruit would be grown. Then, there are the fall feasts: Feast of Trumpets, Atonement, and Tabernacles.

THE SPRING FEASTS

Chapter 3

The Christ in the Passover

Before going into detail about the seven feasts, the Lord first gives instruction about the Sabbath שַׁבָּת. Although it was not seasonal per se, it was continual, and it shadows the end as well (I will expound on this later).

After the Sabbath instructions, the Lord stated: "These are the appointed feasts of the Lord, the holy convocations, which you shall proclaim at the time appointed for them. In the first month, on the fourteenth day of the month at twilight, is the Lord's Passover" (Leviticus 23:4-5 ESV). Considering the Jewish calendar uses a lunisolar system, where months are counted based on the cycle of the moon and years are counted based on the solar cycle, the feasts will change each year slightly. In the Gregorian calendar (the western world's calendar system), the Feast of Passover would fall anywhere between late March and mid-April.

The Passover (Pesach הָעַרְבָּיִם פֶּסַח) feast started in Exodus 12 before God sent the last plague to Egypt.

We read this about the Passover,

> *"The Lord said to Moses and Aaron in the land of Egypt, 'This month shall be for you the beginning of months. It shall be the first month of the year for you. Tell all the congregation of Israel that on the tenth day of this month every man shall take a lamb according to their fathers' houses, a lamb for a household. And if the household is too small for a lamb, then he and his nearest neighbor shall take according to the number of persons; according to what each can eat you shall make your count for the lamb. Your lamb shall be without blemish, a male a year old. You may take it from the sheep or from the goats, and you shall keep it until the fourteenth day of this month, when the whole assembly of the congregation of Israel shall kill their lambs at twilight.*
>
> *'Then they shall take some of the blood and put it on the two doorposts and the lintel of the houses in which they eat it. They shall eat the flesh that night, roasted on the fire; with unleavened bread and bitter herbs they shall eat it. Do not eat any of it raw or boiled in water, but roasted, its head with its legs and its inner parts. And you shall let none of it remain until the morning; anything that remains until the morning you shall burn. In this manner you shall eat it: with your belt fastened, your sandals on your feet, and your staff in your hand. And you shall eat it in haste. It is the Lord's Passover. For I will pass*

through the land of Egypt that night, and I will strike all the firstborn in the land of Egypt, both man and beast; and on all the gods of Egypt I will execute judgments: I am the Lord. The blood shall be a sign for you, on the houses where you are. And when I see the blood, I will pass over you, and no plague will befall you to destroy you, when I strike the land of Egypt"' (Exodus 12:1-13).

The Passover feast was a commemoration of what God did for the children of Israel and it also pointed them to the future when God Himself would be their Passover lamb. John, in the Gospel of John, gives us a precise time when this meeting between God and man took place. There had been many Passovers that Jesus experienced in His life here on earth, but the one that John mentions is the fulfillment of the moedim מְוֹעֲדִים.

John begins the final week of Jesus' life with what is known as the Triumphal Entry. During this time, Jesus rides humbly into Jerusalem on a donkey fulfilling the prophetic words of Zechariah.

"Rejoice greatly, O daughter of Zion! Shout aloud, O daughter of Jerusalem! Behold, your king is coming to you; righteous and having salvation is he, humble and mounted on a donkey, on a colt, the foal of a donkey" (Zechariah 9:9 ESV).

Beyond the fulfillment of Zechariah's prophetic proclamation, this moment was what the children of Israel rehearsed for. For nearly 1,600 years they had taken a lamb, brought it into their home for four days, and then slayed it. Similarly, Jesus, as the Lamb of God (John 1:29), was taken into Jerusalem by the children of Israel for four days then crucified on the cross for the sins of the world.

Just as the blood on the doorposts stopped the spirit of death from entering, so the blood of Jesus delivers us from the power of death and sin and allows those who abide under the blood of Jesus to one day cross over into eternity with God. Paul, when speaking about this triumph for believers, wrote,

> *"When the perishable puts on the imperishable, and the mortal puts on immortality, then shall come to pass the saying that is written: "Death is swallowed up in victory." "O death, where is your victory? O death, where is your sting?" The sting of death is sin, and the power of sin is the law. But thanks be to God, who gives us the victory through our Lord Jesus Christ" (1 Corinthians 15:54-57 ESV).*

During the Feast of Passover, the children of Israel would also eat unleavened bread. This is significant because on many occasions, Jesus compared Himself to bread. Even his birthplace, Bethlehem (בֵּית לֶחֶם), means "house of bread".

When responding to a crowd that was comparing His ministry to that of Moses, Jesus once said, "'I am the bread of life; whoever comes to me shall not hunger, and whoever believes in me shall never thirst'" (John 6:35). In saying this, He was indicating to the crowd that they need to view Him in the same way they viewed bread or water in the natural realm. Just like bread and water are essential for a person's survival, so Jesus is essential for humanity's eternal destination.

On the last Passover before Jesus died, He made sure that the children of Israel understood what they had been rehearsing for. The Bible says, "And he took bread, and when he had given thanks, he broke it and gave it to them, saying, 'This is my body, which is given for you. Do this in remembrance of me'" (Luke 22:19 ESV). The bread He took was the unleavened bread.

Lastly, Jesus directly connected Himself to unleavened bread when He took it and broke it. He showed the disciples that in the same way He just broke the bread, His body must be broken on the cross for the world. Unleavened bread, therefore, is incredibly significant as it relates to Jesus' ministry.

Chapter 4

The Unleavened Bread and Jesus Christ

The next feast is the Feast of Unleavened Bread (Chag HaMatzot חַג הַמַּצּוֹת). The Feast of Unleavened Bread, in our modern calendar, would be celebrated anytime between late March and mid-April.

> *"And on the fifteenth day of the same month is the Feast of Unleavened Bread to the Lord; for seven days you shall eat unleavened bread. On the first day you shall have a holy convocation; you shall not do any ordinary work. But you shall present a food offering to the Lord for seven days. On the seventh day is a holy convocation; you shall not do any ordinary work "(Leviticus 23:6-8 ESV).*

When the children of Israel were coming out of Egypt, God told them through Moses that they were to make bread without leaven and eat it with bitter herbs. The bread was to be made without leaven as a symbol that the Israelites had to leave Egypt quickly. It was also supposed to symbolize to them that life under slavery was bitter, but that God delivered them so that they could be set apart for Him (Exodus 12:8-11).

Paul, in his first letter to the church in Corinth, used the Feast of Unleavened Bread to articulate to the church that they were to be like the unleavened bread. He was appalled by the Corinthian church's passive response to sexual sin in their church (one of their congregants was in a relationship with his father's wife) (1 Corinthians 5:1-6). He addressed this, stating,

> "Cleanse out the old leaven that you may be a new lump, as you really are unleavened. For Christ, our Passover lamb, has been sacrificed. Let us therefore celebrate the festival, not with the old leaven, the leaven of malice and evil, but with the unleavened bread of sincerity and truth" (1 Corinthians 5:7-8 ESV).

Paul painted a clear picture of what the old leaven stood for, which is the sinful nature of man. The statement "cleanse out the old leaven" correlates with the instructions given by Moses. Moses said to the people,

> "Remember this day in which you came out from Egypt, out of the house of slavery, for by a strong hand the Lord brought you out from this place. No leavened bread shall be eaten..."Unleavened bread shall be eaten for seven days; no leavened bread shall be seen with you, and no leaven shall be seen with you in all your territory" (Exodus 13:3,7 ESV).

When the Feast of Unleavened Bread was celebrated in the Old Testament, there was a complete cleansing of leaven from every home and every town they inhabited during this feast.

Likewise, Jesus' symbolized leaven when he became sin for us. "God made him who had no sin to be sin for us, so that in him we might become the righteousness of God" (2 Corinthians 5:21 NIV). As the leaven was to be put out of the homes of the people of God, so Jesus was crucified outside the city (Hebrews 13:12).

Likewise, in the same way the Feast of Unleavened Bread celebrated being set free from the bondage of slavery, Jesus' death meant deliverance from sin and the one who held the power of death,

> "Since therefore the children share in flesh and blood, he himself likewise partook of the same things, that through death he might destroy the one who has the power of death, that is, the devil, and deliver all those who through fear of death were subject to lifelong slavery" (Hebrews 2:14-15 ESV).

When we accept that Jesus died on the cross for us and rose again, it causes us to be set apart, to be holy (1 Peter 2:9; 1 Corinthians 6:11). Paul beautifully compares being set apart with the unleavened bread when he states, "Cleanse out the old leaven that you may be a new lump, as you really are unleavened" (1 Corinthians 5:7 ESV). Indeed, through Christ we can be like the unleavened bread, a people freed from the corruption of sin, delivered from the power of death, and who have entered God's rest.

Chapter 5

Jesus and the Sabbath

The feasts were not the only periods of time that shadowed Christ. Every seventh day of the week, the children of Israel were commanded to rest. This rest is known as the Sabbath, and it too foreshadowed Christs first coming and future return. Therefore, I believe Jesus was buried during two consecutive Sabbaths.

To understand the time of Jesus' burial, one must unravel the biblical story of the burial and resurrection of Jesus Christ. Many scholars agree that according to the Hebrew calendar, Jesus died on the 14th of Nisan, which in our calendar would be the 10th of April. However, the actual day of the week He died is an issue that many dispute. As we unravel the story, let us see if we can pinpoint the exact day. [2]

John stated,

> *"Since it was the day of Preparation, and so that the bodies would not remain on the cross on the Sabbath (for that Sabbath was a high*

day), the Jews asked Pilate that their legs might be broken and that they might be taken away" (John 19:31 ESV).

According to this passage, the day Jesus was crucified was also known as the "day of preparation", which meant they were getting ready for the first day of the Feast of Unleavened Bread. Since the first day of the Feast of Unleavened Bread was commissioned by God to be a Sabbath, they had to get Jesus and the two thieves off the cross before the day was over.

Now, one must understand Jewish people's view of how a normal day functioned to comprehend why they wanted them off the cross around 3 pm. In Genesis, Moses wrote of what a day consisted of: "...And there was evening and there was morning, the first day" (Genesis 1:5). For the rest of the world, a new day begins in the morning (midnight); *however, according to Genesis 1, the evening is the beginning of the day for Jewish people.* So, Jesus and the thieves had to be taken off the cross before Sabbatical first day of the Feast of Unleavened Bread commenced that evening.

When Jesus talked about how long He was going to be buried, He stated: "For just as Jonah was three days and three nights in the belly of the great fish, so will the Son of Man be three days and three nights in the heart of the earth" (Matthew 12:40). According to what Jesus said about Jonah and Himself, one must conclude that when He dies, Jesus must be in His tomb for three days and three nights.

Mark wrote that Jesus died at 3 pm (Mark 15:25). This means He died on the 14th of Nisan during the end of the day. The Feast of the Unleavened Bread would have started the evening after Jesus died. The Bible tells us that at the beginning of the Feast of Unleavened Bread, one cannot work because it is to be considered a Sabbath (Leviticus 23:6-8). This explains why the women could not put spices and anoint Jesus' body that evening because it was against Jewish law for them to work on the Sabbath.

Since the women could not put the spices on Jesus that evening, they waited until the Sabbath ended and then went to anoint Jesus on the day he rose from the dead.

> *"When the Sabbath was past, Mary Magdalene, Mary the mother of James, and Salome bought spices, so that they might go and anoint him. And very early on the first day of the week, when the sun had risen, they went to the tomb." (Mark 16:1-2)*

If we understand this correctly, it means that the women waited three days before anointing Jesus.

As they arrived at the tomb, they were met with an empty tomb and angelic beings who said to them. "... 'Do not be alarmed. You seek Jesus of Nazareth, who was crucified. He has risen; he is not here. See the place where they laid him'" (Mark 16:6). If Jesus died on a Wednesday like some believe, why then did they not come on Friday to place spices on his body? On the other hand, some believe He died on Friday, but if this is true, then He couldn't have risen from the dead on Sunday, because that wouldn't be three days and three nights. To understand clearly what transpired, we must first understand the Sabbath.

Earlier, I spoke about the Sabbath and that although it was not a feast, it still foreshadowed Christ. The Hebrew writer states, "So then, there remains a Sabbath rest for the people of God, for whoever has entered God's rest has also rested from his works as God did from his" (Hebrews 4:9-10 ESV). Through Jesus we enter this Sabbath rest for He has become our Sabbath.

Jesus expounds on this very concept of Him being like the Sabbath when He spoke to the

Pharisees. One day as Jesus and his disciples were walking through the grain-field on the Sabbath, his disciples became hungry and began to pick some heads of the grain and eat them (Deuteronomy 23:25).

The Pharisees were not happy and believed that Jesus' disciples were breaking the Sabbatical law. In their eyes, the disciples were not following Exodus 34:21. This verse states that during the Sabbath, a person was not supposed to harvest wheat. However, equating plucking wheat for the purpose of eating and plowing wheat for income is a stretch by anyone's imagination. Jesus, being fully aware of their religiosity, gave them a response that pointed them back to Scripture, which ultimately pointed back to Him. He said,

> "... 'Have you not read what David did when he was hungry, and those who were with him: how he entered the house of God and ate the bread of the Presence, which it was not lawful for him to eat nor for those who were with him, but only for the priests? Or have you not read in the Law how on the Sabbath the priests in the temple profane the Sabbath and are guiltless? I tell you, something greater than the temple is here. And if you had known what this means, 'I desire mercy, and not sacrifice,' you would not have condemned the guiltless. For the Son of Man is lord of the Sabbath" (Matthew 12:3-6).

Let us carefully dissect this verse to discover the true meaning. First Jesus states,

"Have you not read what David did when he was hungry, and those who were with him: how he entered the house of God and ate the bread of the Presence, which it was not lawful for him to eat nor those who were with him, but only for the priests?" (Matthew 12:3-4).

Jesus is telling a story about David found in 1 Samuel 21:1-9. David and his men, tired from fleeing from King Saul, headed to Nob to the Priest Ahimelech.

As they arrived, Ahimelech came out to meet David, trembling, because he was afraid for his life. But David said something to him that dissolved his fear. David said to Ahimelech the priest,

"The king has charged me with a matter and said to me, 'Let no one know anything of the matter about which I send you, and with which I have charged you.' I have made an appointment with the young men for such and such a place" (1 Samuel 21:2 ESV).

Afterward, David asked for food and the only thing Ahimelech had was the bread of the Presence that only the priest could eat. Knowing this, why then did Jesus use this as an example to justify the actions of the disciples?

Nowhere in Scripture does it say that you could not pick grain to eat on the Sabbath. This was something the Pharisees added to the words of God, elevating themselves to lords of the Sabbath. But this still does not make the comparison of David's situation and his disciples' actions of equal measure. There must have been something else in Scripture that allowed David to be able to eat the bread of the Presence.

I believe David could eat the bread of the Presence because *God cares more about people who are hurting, being helped, than someone following a portion of the (statutes) to the letter.* For there is no greater law than to love God and your neighbor as yourself (Luke 10:26-28). The Priest Ahimelech had a level of authority to decide scripturally if certain circumstances could be annulled due to the greater commandments, such as love, mercy, kindness, justice for the hurting (Micah 6:8). Jesus, therefore, being a Priest in the order of Melchizedek, a higher priestly lineage than that of Aaron, could likewise pick mercy over sacrifice (Hebrews 5:1-8). Indeed, this is the heart of God because in this situation, mercy triumphs over judgment (James 2:13).

Continuing on, Jesus says, " *Or have you not read in the Law how on the Sabbath the priests in the temple profane the Sabbath and are guiltless? I tell you, something greater than the temple is here" (Matthew 12:5-6).* This statement again is pointing the Pharisees back to the Word of God. According to the Bible, the priests in the temple worked on the Sabbath.

The priests still performed sacrifices that needed to be done in the temple during the Sabbath (Numbers 28:9,10; Ezekiel 46:4,5). However, they remained guiltless because they were in the temple. This point, then, is the assimilation of what Jesus was trying to communicate, which is this: that those that are in Him are free from the Laws' demands because He is the fulfillment of the Law. *"For the Son of Man is lord of the Sabbath" (Matthew 12:8).*

However, this does *not* mean that Jesus came to abolish the Law of God (Matthew 5:17). We still must observe the Sabbath, but it is no longer based on a day, but the leading of the Holy Spirit because Jesus has become our rest. Accordingly, Paul stated,

> *"Therefore let no one pass judgment on you in questions of food and drink, or with regard to a festival or a new moon or a Sabbath. These are a shadow of the things to come,*

but the substance belongs to Christ"
(Colossians 2:16-17 ESV).

How does all this information correlate with Jesus in the tomb? Just like the feasts were a rehearsal for the real thing, so also was the celebration of the Sabbath.

Jesus died before the foundations of the world (1 Peter 1:20; Revelations 13:8). This does not mean He physically died, but rather that God had already set the plan in motion before even Adam and Eve sinned. Therefore, aside from God resting, the Sabbath was also a prophetic proclamation that foreshadowed the day when Jesus would be in the tomb and a representation of the ultimate rest that we would eventually enter through Him.

Since the Sabbath points to Jesus, I believe that Jesus was in the heart of the earth for two consecutive Sabbaths. However, it is hard to be certain about how to count the days and nights Jesus was in the tomb. This is because in some instances, Scripture states that Jesus would resurrect after three days or *after three days and nights* (Mark 8:31; Matthew 12:40). While still in other instances it states he will rise on the third day (Matthew 17:23; Mark 9:31; Luke 9:22).

This can seem very confusing and almost as though it's a contradiction. Thankfully, many scholars have done extensive amounts of work on the subject and given us sound understanding on the matter. Understanding why the New Testament writers sometimes stated *three days and three nights* and other times *after three days* or *on the third day* lies in the cultural interpretation of these two phrases.

When one reads Genesis 42:17-18, 1 Samuel 30:12-13, Esther 4:16; 5:1, and 2 Chronicles 10, you notice that the phrase *after three days, after three days and three nights* and *on the third day* are used interchangeably. "Thus, as awkward as it may sound…living in the 21st century, a person in ancient times could legitimately speak of something occurring "on the third day," "after three days," or after "three days and three nights," yet still be referring to the same exact day". [3] With this understanding established, let us now decipher when Jesus died and rose again.

During the days of Jesus, a part of the day was considered the same as the whole day. Thus, Thursday at 3 pm, when Jesus died, could have possibly been the first day he was in the tomb. Being that the Jewish people considered a day to be from evening to evening, Thursday evening following the death of Jesus, to

Friday evening the next day, would have been the first day of the Feast of Unleavened Bread. This was a high holy day Sabbath, and perhaps the second day and first night Jesus was in the tomb.

Friday evening to Saturday evening would be the regular Sabbath (Mark 16) and credibly the third day and second night Jesus was in the tomb. Lastly, Saturday evening to Sunday morning could have been the third and final night Jesus was in the tomb. A night for the Jewish people started when the sun went down and finished after the sun came up. Jesus, therefore, would have resurrected Sunday morning as the night was finishing.

Mary Magdalene, Mary the mother of James, and Salome possibly bought the spices Saturday after the Sabbath finished at sunset. Since it was dark, they could not, because of robbers, wild animals, and the lack of light, go to the tomb and anoint Jesus. Instead, they would have gone to the tomb Sunday morning on the third day. That Sunday morning that Jesus resurrected, happened to also be the Feast of Firstfruits, the only day the women could legally and safely anoint and place the spices on Jesus.

Chapter 6

Jesus and the Feast of Firstfruits

After the feast of Unleavened Bread, God spoke to Moses about the Feast of Firstfruits (Ḥag ha-Bikkurim or Yom Ha-Bikkurim הַבִּכּוּרִים). The Feast of Firstfruits was celebrated on one day. Celebration of this Feast in our modern-day calendar usually would be toward the end of March to sometimes a little after mid-April.

> *"And the Lord spoke to Moses, saying, '"Speak to the people of Israel and say to them, When you come into the land that I give you and reap its harvest, you shall bring the sheaf of the firstfruits of your harvest to the priest, and he shall wave the sheaf before the Lord, so that you may be accepted. On the day after the Sabbath the priest shall wave it. And on the day when you wave the sheaf, you shall offer a male lamb a year old without blemish as a burnt offering to the Lord. And the grain offering with it shall be two tenths of an ephah of fine flour mixed with oil, a food offering to the Lord with a pleasing aroma, and the drink offering with it shall be of wine, a fourth of a hin. And you shall eat neither bread nor grain parched or fresh until this same day, until you have brought the offering*

of your God: it is a statute forever throughout your generations in all your dwellings" (Leviticus 23:9-14 ESV).

My father-in-law is a farmer, and at times he would tell me stories of God protecting his crops. There were times when a hailstorm would come and hit everything around his crops and not a single crop of his would be damaged. He realized early on that although a man may prepare the land, without the right conditions, there will still be no crops.

In the same manner, the Feast of Firstfruits was a time when the children of Israel acknowledged that the only reason there is a harvest is because of God. This acknowledgment was done by them bringing the first cut of their barley to God. The simple application for us today could be giving a tenth of our paychecks to God first. As we do this, we acknowledge that although we may have done the work, God supplied the health and the job, for the earth and all that is in it belongs to God (Psalm 24:1).

Like the other feasts, the Feast of Firstfruits was done to prepare the Israelites for Jesus, who is the first fruit from the dead. This means that Jesus was the first person to resurrect from the dead and to enter Heaven. Paul, addressed this, stating, "But in fact Christ has been raised from the dead, the firstfruits of those who have fallen asleep" (1 Corinthians 15:20 ESV)."

Prior to Jesus' resurrection from the dead, everyone who died in the Old Testament never entered Heaven, but instead went to a place called sheol (ăbaddôn 'destruction,' the pit or Abraham's Bosom) (Numbers 16:30-33; Deuteronomy 32:22; Ezekiel 32:26-27; Job 7:9-10; 10:21; Psalm 88:10; Luke 16:22; Acts 2:27,30). But after Jesus resurrected from the dead, the Bible says,

> *"The tombs also were opened. And many bodies of the saints who had fallen asleep were raised, and coming out of the tombs after his resurrection they went into the holy city and appeared to many" (Matthew 27:52-53 ESV).*

At times, Jesus would compare harvesting to winning souls in the Kingdom of God. He demonstrated this when He saw a crowd that came to hear Him preach and He had compassion on them,

> *"...because they were harassed and helpless, like sheep without a shepherd. Then he said to his disciples, "The harvest is plentiful, but the laborers are few; therefore pray earnestly to the Lord of the harvest to send out laborers into his harvest"' (Matthew 9:36-38 ESV).*

Jesus himself became a symbol of a harvested soul. Symbolically, He became the first fruit of the harvest, like the barley that they brought in Leviticus, when He brought Himself into Heaven. Sin kept every soul out of heaven, which is why everyone who died before Christ could not enter Heaven. Upon His resurrection, Jesus ascended as the first fruit from the dead, a lamb without blemish. Consequently, when speaking to Mary Magdalene, Jesus said, "'Do not cling to me, for I have not yet ascended to the Father; but go to my brothers and say to them, 'I am ascending to my Father and your Father, to my God and your God'" (John 20:17 ESV).

As the first fruit, Jesus could not be even touched by a human being because they were still unclean from sin's corruption. This corruption was finally dealt with when He entered Heaven's courts and presented Himself as the Lamb without blemish, a pleasing aroma to God and the first fruit of those who had fallen asleep. When Jesus entered Heaven, it was not just for the Jews but for the entire world (1 John 2:1-3). Due to this, the next feast after the Feast of Firstfruit is the Feast of Pentecost.

Chapter 7

The Feast of Weeks and the Holy Spirit

Following the Feast of Firstfruits was the Feast of Weeks (Shavuot חַג שָׁבֻעֹת), or as many of us know it, Pentecost. Pentecost, like the Feast of Firstfruits, was celebrated on one day. In our modern-day calendar, the Feast of Pentecost sometimes will fall anytime between late May or early June.

The Lord states,

"'You shall count seven full weeks from the day after the Sabbath, from the day that you brought the sheaf of the wave offering. You shall count fifty days to the day after the seventh Sabbath. Then you shall present a grain offering of new grain to the Lord. You shall bring from your dwelling places two loaves of bread to be waved, made of two tenths of an ephah. They shall be of fine flour, and they shall be baked with leaven, as firstfruits to the Lord. And you shall present with the bread seven lambs a year old without blemish, and one bull from the herd and two rams. They shall be a burnt offering to the Lord, with their grain offering and their drink offerings, a food offering with a pleasing aroma to the Lord. And you shall offer one

male goat for a sin offering, and two male lambs a year old as a sacrifice of peace offerings. And the priest shall wave them with the bread of the firstfruits as a wave offering before the Lord, with the two lambs. They shall be holy to the Lord for the priest. And you shall make a proclamation on the same day. You shall hold a holy convocation. You shall not do any ordinary work. It is a statute forever in all your dwelling places throughout your generations. And when you reap the harvest of your land, you shall not reap your field right up to its edge, nor shall you gather the gleanings after your harvest. You shall leave them for the poor and for the sojourner: I am the Lord your God"'(Leviticus 23:15-22 ESV).

The Feast of Passover indicated the beginning of the barley harvest while the Feast of Pentecost was celebrated during the harvest of wheat. The seven weeks that they were to count started on the Feast of Firstfruits. The total number of days that they counted was fifty (in Greek the word *pente* means fifty).

Unlike the other spring feasts that were celebrated on multiple days, this feast was to be celebrated on one day: the fiftieth day. While I was in Israel, our guide spoke to us about the Feast of Pentecost. He talked about how many of the sages and new Jewish scholars believed that the first feast of Pentecost occurred in the month of Sivan (May-June) during the time when the Ten Commandments were given by God.

One can know the month God came down on Mount Sinai by reading Exodus 19:1. Moses writes, "On the first day of the third month after the Israelites left Egypt—on that very day—they came to the Desert of Sinai" (Exodus 19:1 NIV). The third month in the Jewish calendar is the month of Sivan.

During this first Pentecost in Exodus, God Himself spoke to the people and gave them the Ten Commandments. As God descended upon the mountain, Moses stated, "Now Mount Sinai was wrapped in smoke because the Lord had descended on it in fire. The smoke of it went up like the smoke of a kiln, and the whole mountain trembled greatly" (Exodus 19:18 ESV). The people saw God from afar and witnessed the fire on the mountain.

Some Jewish scholars suggest that God's voice was seen as well as heard on Mount Sinai. The reason for this belief is because in Exodus 20:18, the Hebrew "העם ראים את הקולת" can be translated as "...all the people are seeing the voices, and the flames...".[4] As God spoke, lightning and thunder (which can be translated as flames of fire) were seen. When speaking about God's voice David wrote, "The voice of the Lord flashes forth flames of fire" (Psalm 29:7 ESV).

As with the other feasts, Jesus' life was also the fulfillment of the Feast of Pentecost. This is evidenced by the fact that God commanded the Israelites to bring a new grain offering (Leviticus 23:16) In the New Testament, Jesus *became* our new grain offering. Before going to the cross, Jesus said, "Truly, truly, I say to you, unless a grain of wheat falls into the earth and dies, it remains alone; but if it dies, it bears much fruit" (John 12:24 ESV).

Secondly, during the Feast of Pentecost, the children of Israel brought two loaves of bread for a wave offering (Leviticus 23:17). What do the loaves of bread symbolize? In the New Testament Jesus says He is the true bread that came down from Heaven (John 6:31-35), meaning He was the Word of God manifested. Considering this, the two loaves could symbolize the Old and New Testament which were fully completed by Jesus' life!

Through Jesus' sacrifice, there is now peace between God and man. "For in him all the fullness of God was pleased to dwell, and through Him to reconcile to Himself all things, whether on earth or in heaven, making peace by the blood of His cross" (Colossians 1:19-20 ESV). He fulfilled the peace offering between God and man (Leviticus 23:18-19).

Furthermore, the Holy Spirit's descent upon the disciples in the book of Acts correlates with God's descent upon Mt. Sinai.

The Bible states,

"When the day of Pentecost arrived, they were all together in one place. And suddenly there came from heaven a sound like a mighty rushing wind, and it filled the entire house where they were sitting. And divided tongues as of fire appeared to them and rested on each one of them. And they were all filled with the Holy Spirit and began to speak in other tongues as the Spirit gave them utterance" (Acts 2:1-4 ESV).

Like in Exodus 19, God shows up in the likeness of a fire. The Israelites had to stay far away from the mountain God descended on; however, in the New Testament, people are drawn close because of the sacrifice of Jesus Christ.

The beauty of this feast is that it reminds the Israelites of their mission, which was to be a light to the nations and take care of the hurting and broken. This is why I believe God told them

> "…when you reap the harvest of your land, you shall not reap your field right up to its edge, nor shall you gather the gleanings after your harvest. You shall leave them for the poor and for the sojourner: I am the Lord your God'" (Leviticus 23:22 ESV).

The inclusion of the sojourners, also known as the Gentiles, highlighted the Israelites' purpose, which was to be a kingdom of priests who were to build a bridge between God and man (Exodus 19:6).

Reaching the Gentiles had always been the heart of God. This would finally be fulfilled through God's Son, Jesus. Paul wrote about the fulfillment of this mission in his letter to the church in Ephesus,

> "But now in Christ Jesus you who once were far off have been brought near by the blood of Christ. For he himself is our peace, who has made us both one and has broken down in his flesh the dividing wall of hostility by abolishing the law of commandments expressed in ordinances, that he might create in himself one new man in place of the two, so making peace, and might reconcile us both to God in one body through the cross, thereby killing the hostility. And he came and preached peace to you who were far off and peace to those who were near. For through

him we both have access in one Spirit to the Father. So then you are no longer strangers and aliens, but you are fellow citizens with the saints and members of the household of God…" (Ephesians 2:13-19 ESV).

Chapter 8

The Summer and Testing

After the spring feasts came a three-month period that we call summer (early June-early September). Toward the end of the summer period, during biblical times, the Israelites would harvest fruit. This included grapes, olives, dates, figs, pomegranates and other fruits, seeds, and vegetables.[5]

It is amazing how this all relates to our spiritual life. Pentecost marked the beginning of the harvesting of souls. Each soul won over to God must undergo a period of testing, and one can view the summer as that time of testing. At the end of the testing period the only way you know you have passed the test is if your fruit is ripe (mature).

Our job as believers, therefore, is to be connected to the vine and bear much fruit. Prior to being crucified, Jesus spoke meticulously to the disciples about bearing fruit.

"I am the true vine, and my Father is the vinedresser. Every branch in me that does not bear fruit he takes away, and every branch that does bear fruit he prunes, that it may bear more fruit. Already you are clean Because of the word that I have spoken to you. Abide in me, and I in you. As the branch cannot bear fruit by itself, unless it abides in the vine, neither can you, unless you abide in me. I am the vine; you are the branches. Whoever abides in me and I in him, he it is that bears much fruit, for apart from me you can do nothing. If anyone does not abide in me he is thrown away like a branch and withers; and the branches are gathered, thrown into the fire, and burned. If you abide in me, and my words abide in you, ask whatever you wish, and it will be done for you. By this my Father is glorified, that you bear much fruit and so prove to be my disciples. (John 15: 5-8)

According to what Jesus said, the one who abides in Him will eventually bear fruit because He is the vine. His Father, who Jesus says is the vinedresser, will prune the branches that they may bear much fruit. Pruning, in this case, means to cut the dead parts of the branches off so that there will be new growth.

This process of pruning can be likened to the testing and trials a believer must go through to be refined. The concept of testing by God is highlighted in Proverbs when Solomon states, "The crucible is for silver, and the furnace is for gold, and the LORD tests hearts" (Proverbs 17:3 ESV).

For silver and gold to be refined, they must go through immense heat. Only when the silver and gold have been melted down to their liquid forms can someone remove impurities. Likewise, God uses trials as a furnace in people's lives. As the impurities in the silver and gold rise to the surface when under intense heat, so are the desires from the depths of our hearts revealed through trial. Peter puts it this way, "Beloved, do not be surprised at the fiery trial when it comes upon you to test you, as though something strange were happening to you" (1 Peter 4:12 ESV). Through trials, God searches our hearts and exposes the hidden motives within them. "But I, the LORD, search all hearts and examine secret motives. I give all people their due rewards, according to what their actions deserve" (Jeremiah 17:10 NLT).

Clearly, God will put all believers through tests. However, these tests are not to be mistaken with temptation, for God tempts no one (James 1:13). God's test reveals the condition of a person's heart. Temptation on the other hand, deceives your heart by compelling you to selfishly desire more.

The only way to pass these tests is to abide in Jesus, since He knows the correct answers. The passing grade for our tests we will face is the fruit that is manifested through us. What type of fruit am I talking about? In the book of Galatians, we read about the fruit produced by a life that abides in the Spirit of God.

The author of the book of Galatians was Paul the Apostle. He wrote this letter to the church in Galatia, which is in modern-day Turkey. Throughout the book of Galatians, Paul emphasized the fact that a person is saved and justified through faith. This is because there were some among the believers in Galatia who argued that a person needed the law in order for them to be truly saved.

Paul, on the other hand, rebuked this thought process and told the church in Galatia, "For if you are trying to make yourselves right with God by keeping the law, you have been cut off from Christ! You have fallen away from God's grace" (Galatians 5:4). Paul believed individuals would be cut off from Christ because apart from the Spirit of God, we are under the control of our fleshly nature.

This fleshly nature does not desire the things of God. Consequently, it is of no use to try to be saved through the Law because the Law is perfect and we are not. Therefore, when a sinful man attempts to fulfill a perfect Law they are imprisoned by the Law because like a mirror, it shows them all their shortcomings and causes them to be condemned (Galatians 2; Galatians 3).

The only conclusion to truly being saved and justified is through someone who could accomplish the Law and adopt us into His family. This is exactly what Paul addresses when he said,

> "In the same way we also, when we were children, were enslaved to the elementary principles of the world. But when the fullness of time had come, God sent forth his Son, born of woman, born under the law, to redeem those who were under the law, so that we might receive adoption as sons. And because you are sons, God has sent the Spirit of his Son into our hearts, crying, 'Abba! Father!' So you are no longer a slave, but a son, and if a son, then an heir through God" (Galatians 4:3-7 ESV).

Through Jesus Christ, we now can truly have a free will. Previously, the power of sin governed our bodies and we walked in the flesh; now, through the Spirit of God, we can choose to walk in the flesh or the Spirit. "For freedom Christ has set us free; stand firm therefore, and do not submit again to a yoke of slavery" (Galatians 5:1 ESV). It is in submitting our freedom to Christ that we truly can walk in the spirit and not gratify the desires of the flesh.

When we choose to submit to the Spirit, Paul explains that the evidence of this submission should be shown by fruit that's produced in our lives by the Holy Spirit. Paul says, "But the fruit of the Spirit is love, joy, peace, patience, kindness, goodness, faithfulness, gentleness, self-control; against such things there is no law" (Galatians 5:22-23 ESV).
All these manifestations of the one Spirit are subsumed and expressed through love (1 Corinthians 13). In other words, it's one fruit with different aspects; a multifaceted fruit. Therefore, a person cannot say they have joy and not love. Joy is a characteristic of love, and love is the capsule of the fruit of the Spirit.

This is the fruit Jesus will be inspecting one day when we stand before Him. This is why during the time of testing (summer) that we are in now, it's important to yield our lives to the Holy Spirit. Only when we surrender everything to the Holy Spirit will we truly walk in the Spirit.

Unfortunately, not everyone is willing to surrender their lives to the Holy Spirit. And because of their unwillingness to allow Jesus to have full control of their lives, one day they may be separated from Jesus for eternity. Jesus says, *"If anyone does not abide in me he is thrown away like a branch and withers; and the branches are gathered, thrown into the fire, and burned" (John 15:6).* This process of separation and judgment is what the next three feasts will address. The spring feasts were about Jesus first coming; the fall feasts are about Jesus' return!

THE FALL FEASTS

Chapter 9

Jesus and the Feast of Trumpets

The number seven is a significant number in Scripture. From Genesis to Revelation, we see this number repeated. The first mention of it is in Genesis when it says,

> *"And on the seventh day God finished his work that he had done, and he rested on the seventh day from all his work that he had done. So God blessed the seventh day and made it holy, because on it God rested from all his work that he had done in creation"* *(Genesis 2:2-3).*

This is the first Sabbath, a day of commemorating what God had done and to rest as He did.

Thus, in accordance with this passage, the seventh day can signify rest and completion. From this foundational understanding we can infer that when we see the number seven throughout the Bible, it likewise reflects rest and completion. The Hebrew writer used the seventh day to illustrate us entering Heaven one day. He stated,

> "So then, there remains a Sabbath rest for the people of God, for whoever has entered God's rest has also rested from his works as God did from his. Let us therefore strive to enter that rest, so that no one may fall by the same sort of disobedience" (Hebrews 4:9-11 ESV).

Keeping this in mind, one can get a better understanding of the fall feasts that all take place on the seventh month. The first of these three feasts is the Feast of Trumpets (Rosh Hashanah, Yom Teruah יוֹם תְּרוּעָה). God says this to Moses regarding this feast:

> "...Speak to the people of Israel, saying, In the seventh month, on the first day of the month, you shall observe a day of solemn rest, a memorial proclaimed with a blast of trumpets, a holy convocation. You shall not do any ordinary work, and you shall present a food offering to the Lord'" (Leviticus 23:23-25 ESV).

The seventh month in the Jewish calendar is the month called Tishri. In our calendar, this month would fall somewhere between the month of September through October.

The seventh month was only called Tishri after the exile from Babylon, it means "beginning". Originally, the name for the seventh month was *Ethanim*, meaning "perennials".[6] A perennial is a plant that is present at all seasons of the year.[7]

Biblically, the original name for the seventh month is only mentioned once amid the dedication of Solomon's temple (1 Kings 8:2 ESV). This story is also found in 2 Chronicles 5 and it describes the tangible glory of God falling on the temple Solomon built.

God does nothing coincidentally; everything He does has a purpose. Notice how it is in the seventh month, a sabbatical month, that the tangible glory of God falls on the temple. The month, named Perennials, is the month that the eternal God, who is the beginning and brings life everlasting, decides to come and enter the temple Solomon built.

From the beginning, God set aside the seventh month as a month that would foreshadow His return, when everything would be completed, and we would enter His rest. The first feast in this month is the Feast of Trumpets. I believe when Paul is speaking about the end times to the Church in Corinth, he shares something that is reflective of this feast:

> *"Behold! I tell you a mystery. We shall not all sleep, but we shall all be changed, in a moment, in the twinkling of an eye, at the last trumpet. For the trumpet will sound, and the dead will be raised imperishable, and we shall be changed" (1 Corinthians 15:51-52 ESV).*

Many scholars say that what Paul is talking about here is the rapture, which means "to be caught up." Paul further describes this when talking to the church in Thessalonica about the end times. He tells them,

> *"For this we declare to you by a word from the Lord, that we who are alive, who are left until the coming of the Lord, will not precede those who have fallen asleep. For the Lord himself will descend from heaven with a cry of command, with the voice of an archangel, and with the sound of the trumpet of God. And the dead in Christ will rise first. Then we who are alive, who are left, will be caught up together with them in the clouds to meet the Lord in the air, and so we will always be with the Lord" (1 Thessalonians 4:15-17 ESV).*

One day Heaven will blast its trumpet and those who belong to God, who bore fruit through trials, will be gathered by the angels, and saved from the day of God's wrath. On the other hand, those whose sins have not been atoned for on that day will experience eternal separation from God. Henceforth, the next feast after the Feast of Trumpets is the Day of Atonement!

Chapter 10

The Day of Atonement and God's Wrath

There was one day of the year when the high priest would enter the Holy of Holies and make a sacrifice for the whole nation of Israel (Hebrews 9:7). That day was known as Yom (יוֹם) meaning 'day' in Hebrew and Kippur (כִּפּוּר) translated as ' atonement,' the Day of Atonement.

God says this to Moses about the Day of Atonement,

> *"'Now on the tenth day of this seventh month is the Day of Atonement. It shall be for you a time of holy convocation, and you shall afflict yourselves and present a food offering to the Lord. And you shall not do any work on that very day, for it is a Day of Atonement, to make atonement for you before the Lord your God. For whoever is not afflicted on that very day shall be cut off from his people. And whoever does any work on that very day, that person I will destroy from among his people. You shall not do any work. It is a statute forever throughout your generations in all your dwelling places. It shall be to you a Sabbath of solemn rest, and you shall afflict yourselves. On the ninth day of the month*

beginning at evening, from evening to evening shall you keep your Sabbath" (Leviticus 23:27-32 ESV).

Out of all the feasts, the Day of Atonement is the only one where God says that *they should afflict themselves*. The seriousness of this day can be felt just from reading about it.

On one of my trips to Israel I went to the Temple Institute, a place where Orthodox Jews prepare items for the rebuilding of the temple and learned about what many of the Jews believed would happen during Yom Kippur. It has been a pervasive thought that on the Day of Atonement, the Final Judgment will be issued. As a result, God placed such great emphasis during this feast on repentance, which was turning away from one's sins and turning to God.

Jesus is our great High Priest and,

"Unlike the other high priests, he does not need to offer sacrifices day after day, first for his own sins, and then for the sins of the people. He sacrificed for their sins once for all when he offered himself" (Hebrews 4:14-16; Hebrews 7:27).

Through His sacrifice He has appeased the wrath of God (1 John 2:1-4). Yet the one who does not believe remains under the wrath of God (John 3:36).

One day God will judge the entire world. God flooded the earth with water in the time of Noah, but one day He will consume it with fire. Peter the Apostle explained it this way:

> *"But the day of the Lord will come like a thief, and then the heavens will pass away with a roar, and the heavenly bodies will be burned up and dissolved, and the earth and the works that are done on it will be exposed" (2 Peter 3:10 ESV).*

We need to understand, though, that God does not celebrate judgment. God wants everyone to repent and none to perish (2 Peter 3:9). This can be seen when Jesus, who is the image of the invisible God (Colossians 1:15), wept over Jerusalem when they did not know their hour of visitation and were going to face judgment. Luke, when writing about this says,

> *"And when he drew near and saw the city, he wept over it, saying, "Would that you, even you, had known on this day the things that make for peace! But now they are hidden from your eyes. For the days will come upon you, when your enemies will set up a barricade around you and surround you and hem you in on every side and tear you down to the ground, you and your children within you. And they will not leave one stone upon another in you, because you did not know the time of your visitation"' (Luke 19:41-44 ESV).*

Moses once went up Mount Sinai to get instructions on how to prepare a place for us to dwell with God and receive the written commandments of God. When he left, he placed Aaron (his brother) and other leaders over the people. He was not gone longer than forty days and those who remained on the base of the mountain rebelled (Exodus 24-32).

When he came down from the mountain he burned with anger. The Bible says,

> *"And as soon as he came near the camp and saw the calf and the dancing, Moses' anger burned hot, and he threw the tablets out of his hands and broke them at the foot of the mountain. He took the calf that they had made and burned it with fire and ground it to powder and scattered it on the water and made the people of Israel drink it" (Exodus 32:19-20 ESV).*

Just prior to the forty days that Moses went up Mount Sinai, the elders all encountered God and ate within His proximity (Exodus 24 ESV). But in just over a month, all their experiences were forgotten as these very elders reverted to their old ways of living.

Their disobedience caused many to perish as brother had to kill brother, friends killed friends, and neighbor killed neighbor with the sword (Exodus 32:26-30). Thousands died during this judgment and there was a clear separation between those who were for God and those who were not. The Levi's, the true priests, were set apart on this day.

Jesus, likewise, has also climbed the Mountain of God (Psalm 24:3-4). He is preparing a place for us to dwell with God like Moses did (John 14:3). One day, He also like Moses will return (Acts 1:11). Many will also perish on the day of His return, and the true priests will be revealed (Matthew 25:31-46).

Jesus will come into Jerusalem and reign with an iron scepter (Revelation 2:27). As He is reining, those who were separated will reign with him (Revelation 20:4-6). This will be the fulfillment of the last feast, the Feast of Tabernacles.

Chapter 11

The Feast of Tabernacles and Jesus' Return

We have already addressed the fact that God decided to reveal himself to the children of Israel in the seventh month, after Solomon had finished building his temple (2 Chronicles 5). This revelation, where the shekinah glory (seen or tangible glory of God) fell on the temple, is also commemorated with a feast. The Bible states, "So all the men of Israel assembled before the king at the annual Festival of Shelters, which is held in early autumn" (2 Chronicles 5:3 NLT).

The Festival of Shelters is also known as the Feast of Tabernacles (Sukkot סֻכּוֹת). Regarding the Feast of Tabernacles, God said this to Moses:

> "'Speak to the people of Israel, saying, On the fifteenth day of this seventh month and for seven days is the Feast of Booths to the Lord. On the first day shall be a holy convocation; you shall not do any ordinary work. For seven days you shall present food offerings to the Lord. On the eighth day you shall hold a holy convocation and present a food offering to the

Lord. It is a solemn assembly; you shall not do any ordinary work.

'On the fifteenth day of the seventh month, when you have gathered in the produce of the land, you shall celebrate the feast of the Lord seven days. On the first day shall be a solemn rest, and on the eighth day shall be a solemn rest. And you shall take on the first day the fruit of splendid trees, branches of palm trees and boughs of leafy trees and willows of the brook, and you shall rejoice before the Lord your God seven days. You shall celebrate it as a feast to the Lord for seven days in the year. It is a statute forever throughout your generations; you shall celebrate it in the seventh month. You shall dwell in booths for seven days. All native Israelites shall dwell in booths, that your generations may know that I made the people of Israel dwell in booths when I brought them out of the land of Egypt: I am the Lord your God'" (Leviticus 23:34-36, 39-43 ESV).

During this feast, even the king would come out of his palace and dwell in a booth and live among the common man. In 2 Chronicles 5 & 6, we see King Solomon doing just that.

After the glory had fallen on the temple, Solomon made this assertion, "But will God indeed dwell with man on the earth? Behold, heaven and the highest heaven cannot contain you, how much less this house that I have built!" (2 Chronicles 6:18). Solomon, having seen the magnificent nature of the glory of God, could not fully fathom God's presence abiding in the temple he built.

In the book of Acts, Paul elaborates more on this fact. When he came to Athens and saw an inscription written to an "unknown god", he began to explain to the people that this "unknown God" was really the God of Heaven. He stated, "The God who made the world and everything in it, being Lord of heaven and earth, does not live in temples made by man…" (Acts 17:24 ESV).

Indeed, God does not live in temples made by man, yet He does live in His temple, which is us. "Do you not know that you are God's temple and that God's Spirit dwells in you? If anyone destroys God's temple, God will destroy him. For God's temple is holy, and you are that temple" (1 Corinthians 3:16-17 ESV). One of God's goals has always been to tabernacle (dwell) with us! As the King would come out of his palace and live amongst the people during the Feast of Tabernacles, God one day will come down from Heaven and dwell with us.

Another name for this feast is the Feast of Ingathering (Exodus 23:16) because it's when the last

of the produce was gathered (Leviticus 23:39).
Likewise, one day there will be an ingathering of all the
souls in the world. As Jesus will come back and reign
here on the earth. This will be known as the Millennial
Reign when Jesus will rule here on earth for 1,000
years (Revelation 19).

Zechariah beautifully writes about the future
Feast of Tabernacles (or Feast of Booths) at the end of
his prophetic book. He starts the final chapter of his
book, chapter 14, by describing the last battle, which is
also known as the Battle of Armageddon (Revelations
16:16). In this last chapter, Zechariah explains how the
nations of the world will be gathered by God to battle
against Jerusalem. Not that God makes these nations
do evil, but that Jerusalem's accumulation of sin leads
them to this final judgment (Zechariah 14:1-4).

These nations will plunder Jerusalem and rape
the women. But like my son dreamt when he was three
years old, Jesus will one day return. Upon His return,
He will stand on the Mount of Olives, and it will split into
two halves (Zechariah 14:4-15). Jesus will begin His
reign at this moment and every nation of every tongue
will be expected to come and celebrate the Feast of

Booths. If not, judgment will come upon them and their nation.

> *"Then everyone who survives of all the nations that have come against Jerusalem shall go up year after year to worship the King, the Lord of hosts, and to keep the Feast of Booths. And if any of the families of the earth do not go up to Jerusalem to worship the King, the Lord of hosts, there will be no rain on them. And if the family of Egypt does not go up and present themselves, then on them there shall be no rain; there shall be the plague with which the Lord afflicts the nations that do not go up to keep the Feast of Booths"* *(Zechariah 14:16-18 ESV).*

These seven feasts were all appointments set up by God. With the first four already accomplished, we must be ready for the last three. I believe we are currently living in the summer season, a time of testing a time when the fruit of our lives must ripen. These are the last days. In Book 2, we will talk more about Daniel's visions and dreams. I believe that as we carefully dissect these dreams and visions, we can gain more insight and understanding about these last three feasts.

References

1. Brown, Francis, S R Driver, Charles A Briggs, Edward Robinson, James, Strong, and Wilhelm Gesenius. 2015. *The Brown, Driver, Briggs Hebrew and English Lexicon: With an Appendix Containing the Biblical Aramaic: Coded with the Numbering System from Strong's Exhaustive Concordance of the Bible.* Peabody, Mass.: Hendrickson Publishers.

2. Anderson, Robert. 2016. *The Coming Prince.* First Rate Publishers.

3. "Did Jesus Rise 'On' or 'After' the Third Day?" n.d. Www.apologeticspress.org. Accessed June 18, 2021. https://www.apologeticspress.org/APContent.aspx?&article=756.

4. Young, Robert. 2015. *Young's Literal Translation of the Holy Bible.*

5. "Harvest Seasons of Ancient Israel." n.d. GCI Archive. Accessed June 18, 2021. https://archive.gci.org/articles/harvest-seasons-of-ancient-israel/.

6. "The Amazing Name Ethanim: Meaning and Etymology." n.d Abarim Publications. Accessed June 18, 2021.

7. "Definition of PERENNIAL." N.d. www.merriam-webster.com. https://www.merriam-webster.com/dictionary/perennial.

www.ingramcontent.com/pod-product-compliance
Lightning Source LLC
Chambersburg PA
CBHW060351050426
42449CB00011B/2919